ROUGH
KNOWLEDGE

ANHINGA PRESS

ROUGH KNOWLEDGE

POEMS

CHRISTINE POREBA

2014 Philip Levine Prize for Poetry

Selected by Peter Everwine

ANHINGA PRESS

TALLAHASSEE, FLORIDA 2016

Cover Image: John Mann "Untitled" from series *Thinner Air*, 2011
Author photograph: John Mann
Design and production: Jay Snodgrass
Type Styles: titles and text set in Minion Pro

Library of Congress Cataloging-in-Publication Data
Rough Knowledge by Christine Poreba — First Edition
ISBN — 978-1-934695-47-0
Library of Congress Cataloging Card Number — 2015947217

Anhinga Press Inc. is a nonprofit corporation dedicated wholly to the
publication and appreciation of fine poetry and other literary genres.

For personal orders, catalogs, and information, write to:

ANHINGA PRESS
P.O. Box 3665 • Tallahassee, Florida 32315
Website: www.anhingapress.org • Email: info@anhinga.org

Published in the United States by Anhinga Press
Tallahassee, Florida • First Edition, 2016

for John

THE PHILIP LEVINE PRIZE FOR POETRY

The annual competition for the Philip Levine Prize for Poetry is sponsored and administered by the M.F.A. Program in Creative Writing at California State University, Fresno.

2014
Christine Poreba
Rough Knowledge
Selected by Peter Everwine

2013
Chelsea Wagenaar
Mercy Spurs the Bone
Selected by Philip Levine

2012
Barbara Brinson Curiel
Mexican Jenny and Other Poems
Selected by Cornelius Eady

2011
Ariana Nadia Nash
Instructions for Preparing Your Skin
Selected by Denise Duhamel

2010
Lory Bedikian
The Book of Lamenting
Selected by Brian Turner

2009
Sarah Wetzel
Bathsheba Transatlantic
Selected by Garrett Hongo

2008
Shane Seely
The Snowbound House
Selected by Dorianne Laux

2007
Neil Aitken
The Lost Country of Sight
Selected by C.G. Hanzlicek

2006
Lynn Aarti Chandhok
The View from Zero Bridge
Selected by Corrinne Clegg Hales

2005
Roxane Beth Johnson
Jubilee
Selected by Philip Levine

2002
Steven Gehrke
The Pyramids of Malpighi
Selected by Philip Levine

2001
Fleda Brown
Breathing In, Breathing Out
Selected by Philip Levine

CONTENTS

ACKNOWLEDGMENTS

Grateful acknowledgment is made to the editors and readers of the following journals in which these poems first appeared, sometimes in earlier versions:

Birmingham Poetry Review: "Before Marriage Dream and Waking (No. 1)"
BOXCAR Poetry Review: "Poem of Lost Lines"
Florida Review: "Through Elements"
La Fovea: "Flight"
Limestone: "Silent Elegy"
Momoware: "In Nothing Less than One Whole Second"
Natural Bridge: "Alight"
The Pinch: "What You Don't Want to Know"
Poet Lore: "A Short Treatise on Loss"
Potomac Review: "Rebuilding a House"
Rattle: "Unplotted" "Between Missing and Found"
Subtropics: "Courting, Paynes Prairie"
The Southern Review: "A Short History of Leavening," "Last Breath"
The Sow's Ear Poetry Review: "Balcony"
Swarthmore Literary Review: "Remodeling"
Tallahassee Democrat: "This Morning"
Verse Wisconsin: "Woman in a Dream"

The poems "The Turn" (as "Rough Knowledge") and "Even in Clear Air" were awarded a 2011 Prize from the Dorothy Sargent Rosenberg Foundation and appear on their website.

I am very thankful to my family, friends, fellow poets, and teachers; the Virginia Center for the Creative Arts, the Hambidge Center for the Creative Arts and Sciences, and Ragdale Foundation; everyone involved with the Philip Levine Prize at California State University, Fresno; Anhinga Press; and, Peter Everwine, for selecting my manuscript.

I.

TOWARD HOME

My husband and I pass a horseshoe crab on its back,
and I think: another dead thing.

This is the ancient armor my father would pack
in plastic bags every August. I can still smell

the crumbling seaweed, feel the sharp points
of their tails poking me and my sister in the backseat.

I've forgotten whether he ever told us that these husks
were only remnants of one stage of the creatures' lives,

that they would have already been swimming in new skin
as we traveled back from summer.

My husband rights the horseshoe crab,
and, to my surprise, it moves,

like a speeding turtle or a dusty shoe with legs.
If there were music to accompany this dance

of what I thought was dead becoming alive again,
it would have to be the tuba, whose highest notes are held

by their own weight, whose strains of comedy
steep beneath the dark. But just a few feet

from the water's edge, our horseshoe crab stops —
does his eye (one of ten, I learn later)

alert him to the shadows of us, still standing?
Or to the birds, whom I've heard could pluck

his insides out while he is still alive? We wait for him
to move again because we want to see the end,

when he gets back home, to imagine the first
moment that sea streams through his bookgills,

coats his tail, sets his brain in sync again
with the shore's cycles of light and dark.

I think of our own approaching journey,
how in those last few hours on the road it hurts to stop.

We stand and readjust our eyes to keep him
from becoming just another set of tracks in distant sand.

BALCONY

This balcony has a view onto the past
I haven't noticed before this morning
when my father calls down, holds
a spatula stacked with pancakes he keeps
lifting out of the sizzle as he prepares
a pile that will keep him company
while he waits for me to sit with him today.

He calls down to the back bench,
where I used to think I was hiding,
kissing there nights after I'd walked
between the playgrounds,
shuffled around for my key,
decided to stay a little longer
with somebody laughing in my arms.

I look up when my father calls,
wonder that the pancakes don't crash
down, one by one, into the place where I sat,
sit — I don't always know if I am there
or am remembering that I am there;
each metal link between the playgrounds
is so familiar, what I used to go by.

And I want to know if everything happens
twice this way, ends, and starts again —
the pancakes, the kissing, the always looking back.

COURTING, PAYNES PRAIRIE

> *Do you remember, my love,*
> *our first steps on the island?*
> *The gray stones knew us,*
> *the rain squalls,*
> *the shouts of the wind in the shadow.*
>   — Pablo Neruda

In the shadows of a palm grove,
I wait for him to move

closer. He has stumbled
to this bench like the wanderer who fumbled

from Poseidon's wicked pocket
into the solace of an olive thicket.

Now that we sit together,
we can't decide whether,

or when, which of us will touch the other's hand.
All afternoon, we've scanned

the thick, shadowy pond
for alligators, grown fond

of this luminous corner of air
where

red-splattered black flies
gorge on sweet clover's nectar as they rise,

ruthlessly mating
in the midst of our slow waking.

FLIGHT

A butterfly flaps lightly
down the highway.
It's how a prayer
might look when sent
to spoken air.

It floats toward
our windshield,
and is gone.

On the scale of tragedy,
this collision
is a fight in a dollhouse.

But the mark left
on the glass could
look a bit like
any human sorrow —

the way the stain spreads
crooked in a corner,
and vibrant colors slur
into a spot of white
that opens up
another memory,

another butterfly,
one we climbed
to a roof to release
from a box
into the city,

one flying close
to the ground
that a four-year-old
with a purple sneaker
and double-knotted laces
stepped on with a purpose
no one understood, with the force
of a harsh current of sky.

SILENT ELEGY

Your cousin died before I knew you,
when you used to photograph the shadows

of your hand, its weathered palm
shifting like a pendulum.

When she committed suicide at thirty-six,
you started walking through New Mexico's

wooded trails, photographing holes in the earth,
telephone poles that became landmarks

on a little known road.
In your kitchen, you created small accidents:

a pitcher crashing to the floor in slow motion,
its contents pouring out over and over.

LEAVING NEW YORK

My mother and I look out
the window of my childhood
bedroom. Fourteen flights up,
Manhattan is scattered lights;
clusters of buildings, like children
growing, change heights across
the sky. I used to worry,
as a teacher, that I'd lose a child
in this city. I remember waking
in the middle of the night,
feeling certain I had left
one somewhere — on the ferry
to Staten Island, in a cluttered
corner of the classroom.
My mother is always amazed
by the beauty of those lights,
flickering before me
as if from another world:
all those rooftops filled with children
who've forgotten my name.

A KIND OF SINGING

Our dreams, I think, are like birds,
slips of selves pecking at a high window,
trying to get in through a different light.

They arrive in a single yard, brazen,
gathering the scattered seeds.
Birds move when it's time again,

carry nothing but themselves,
as we in our dreams are able to begin
a journey without remembering

the time of departure, without
having with us the essential belongings.
When we fly in sleep, Freud says,

we repeat those games from childhood,
when an aunt or uncle held us
in the air, except now we've lost

their hands and yet float on.
We enter daylight tucked still inside
our own unraveling.

The dream remembered is a stitch of singing.
In it, my young dog becomes the old cat
from my childhood, his red fur turning

tabby before he steps out
onto a snow-covered balcony,
a palimpsest of paw prints.

THE PACE OF THINGS

And now another time had come.
— Wendell Berry

On some street near the white cat's house,
    where we slowed our walking to see if she was there

to scurry to the curb, throw her body on the sidewalk,
    purr and turn as our dog sniffed, wiggling, paw out,

tail wagging, curious for whatever came next,
    I looked up to see only the back of you:

your legs like branches of some other time,
    your back a field, and above the wide distance

from shoulder to shoulder, a little stalk of hair held
    to your whole round head, lifted softly with each step,

and fell again, lifted and fell into the air, again and again
    in a rhythm that most nights on our walk is hidden

as the last parts of ourselves make a quiet phrase
    behind us in the dark. Is this how growing old together goes —

after half a thousand evenings on the same route,
    there'll be still another part of you to see, to know by heart?

A YEAR IN WEATHER

It was the year that summer would not end,
and the year that winter froze the oranges in Florida,
where we left our pipes to drip for two weeks straight.

The year people began asking us if we wanted
to have children, and all we knew to say was,
"We don't know." And then more rain.

Yesterday, it fell hard from a dark sky and a few
students looked nervously out the window,
including the young woman from Haiti who began

my class the day before the earthquake splintered
her island. On one of the days of that ceaseless summer,
I drove to cover for a teacher, whose father

was quickly dying, and passed a marmalade cat
dead in the street, head tucked, paws curled;
overhead, geese flew to another place.

This morning, the man who paces our street,
who sometimes waves his arms in anger at the clouds,
stands still looking up at them, as though he's waiting

for their answer. This morning, the fog is so dense
that children walking to school are ghosts.
Under the vapor, our flowers lie frozen in the brown grass.

IN NOTHING LESS THAN ONE WHOLE SECOND

Pantoum on a Line from Wisława Szymborska

The sound of somebody not arriving
The dog nudging his bowl for a crumb
Bullets flying a thousand miles north
A lone thread of guises is all seconds soon become

The dog nudges his bowl for a last crumb
Barks at the wind swinging no one in
A lone thread of guises is all seconds soon become
The print of a span of wings flown into glass

He barks at the wind swinging no one in
On a road south lies the soft wide back of a dead raccoon
It's the print of a body flown into
Life at the mercy of the trickle of what's left

The soft wide back of a dead raccoon faces south
Trash collectors in Baghdad carry their souls in their hands
We're all at the mercy of the trickle of what leaves us
A goose that was part of the pack headed west is gone

Trash collectors in Baghdad carry souls in their hands
Somebody's fists curled up asleep open in another world
A goose that was part of the pack is gone
Our lives are all wires waiting to catch

Fists curled up asleep open to another world
To the sound of somebody not arriving
To the current of a wire waiting to catch
To the past of a thousand bullets flying

THIS MORNING

A bird paces
along the top

of a traffic light
where I am stopped;

cars rush along,
their windows closed

as his tiny voice
rises and falls.

My heart's always
breaking

at the smallest
of moments.

ON FORGETTING YOU MIGHT NEED A RIDE

You called me but I didn't answer.
My love, I was elsewhere, dizzy in light,
lost in the loropetalum.
The dog dozed with a ball tucked
under his paws. Inside our house,
a cavalcade of doorways sighed.
As if they too loved this quiet.
As if the space they gathered in
were made to contain us.
I want them both:
the space, the containment.
You called me but I didn't answer.
My love, I was elsewhere, lost
in doorways, sighing while the dog
dozed with a ball beside
the loropetalum. I want the space.
I want the containment.
My love, you called me but I didn't
answer. I was dizzy in light, lost
inside our house, the loropetalum,
the cavalcade of doorways;
sighed, I want the expanse and the enfoldment.

How those roses you planted now climb
their pickets, fat white blossoms: belonging, opened.

BEFORE MARRIAGE DREAM AND WAKING (NO. 1)

Last night I flew for hours,
five feet above our lawn,
a simple breaststroke
in the air,

as if all the swimming
I had done
were preparation
for this flight,

the water,
a mantle for this new
bearing of light
and ground.

Awake, I heard
your breathing
and it was the wind
still rising.

Two windows stood
at the foot of our bed,
an entrance to this world
from another view.

And the light
that filtered through
came from a moon
that wouldn't set.

THE THORNE ROOMS

A Collection of Miniature Rooms in the Art Institute of Chicago

History at its most miniature: the world,
but smaller, more privileged, brightened
by tiny bulbs that imitate sunlight

slipping through gauze curtains the size
of checkerboard squares onto dark brown
Shaker floorboards without footprints or dust,

through Venetian blinds thinner than toothpicks,
and across thresholds of delicately carved doorways
with crystal knobs, precise as pencil points,

of a sitting room nobody enters,
where a brass trumpet awaits its player.
On a two-inch tall cherry-wood table

sits a pair of wire-rimmed glasses,
a ball of yarn smaller than a marble,
half-knitted on a needle the length of an eyelash . . .

Is this what the world will look like when we're gone?
Every room its own exquisite universe, emptied
of inhabitants but filled with infinite detail,

seen by a few scattered onlookers, going slowly
to absorb as much as they can, though
only the smallest fraction will ever be remembered.

REBUILDING A HOUSE

You learn words like *soffit*, the underside of eave,
    and *bone pile*, the place misordered parts go,
and that everything must come out:
    the rolled up newspaper from 1966 tucked
into a wall, and the door it covered up,
    an oversized window somebody else once chose,
two bracelets of rusted charms,
    and several planks of gray painted oak,
plucked with surgical precision to be used again.
    When another month comes like wild fire,
still your rooms are empty and an electrician
    with reddened eyes turns up whenever
you don't expect him, when you're staring
    at a fence of half-finished pickets,
or tiptoeing in dirty feet from clock to clock.
    You become as thorough as an expectant mother
explaining to your guest how, once, the room
    she's standing in was nothing more than air.
She politely shakes her head and says,
    "It's difficult to imagine," but you feel the need
to continue to describe how in the spot
    where the chair is now, an open bag
of sunflower seeds once rested on plywood.
    When you read that in Athens,
the two-thousand-year-old Odeon is suffering
    from the consistent ache of women
bearing down on it in stilettos,
    you think you hear the contented sigh
of your own (comparatively new-born) house
    straightening out her pleated skirt.

MODEL AIRPLANE, LATE JULY

I released you and you flew,
into the light of things that were
about to end — evening, summer —

into air beneath mountains;
you whom my husband, crouching
to catch your flight on film, had built.

He'd say, "Ready when you are,"
wait for my hands to loosen their hold,
and there you would go, my lightness,

without pistons or passengers,
with only a rubber band to clamp
those tissue paper wings in place.

You in that breakable skin, driven
by wind, your flight the slant
at which I emptied my hands,

your flight a journey become
an instant. Wherever you landed,
whether after a smooth line of solitude,

or a sudden series of spins, I'd lift
those red plastic petals at your nose,
wind them, and release.

If only other things were this easy to let go,
this graceful in falling. If only every unexpected
turn, mid-journey, were so full of delight.

BEFORE MARRIAGE DREAM (NO. 2)

My grandfather is back
at his old spot, in my old life,
head down at the kitchen table.

Such seasoned steps for a dream
to take — he, ten years dead, returns,
and you, whom he never met,

are the one to tell me he has something
to tell us, and we travel from Tallahassee
to New York in moments to discover

what it is, only to then not discover it
because there he is, just sitting, the way
a child would for a game, waiting to be tapped.

He's somebody else, when he rises,
not a construction worker or army chef,
not the man who would take me to the bakery

after school and tell me to choose anything
I wanted, but somebody dressed in a suit
on his way into an office building, not looking.

Now you're tapping me to say
you can hear my grandmother, who
isn't dead, sing an aria from the top

of a set of spiral stairs. This beloved
voice I've heard all my life sing
Polish songs, like *Sto Lat, Sto Lat,*

Niech żyje, żyje nam, — *May he live*
a hundred years for us, — floats,
unseen, echoing music

that only you can hear, my love.
When it stops, you pause
and I breathe the air

of a world
which one of us
will be first to leave.

SYMPHONY IN THE BRAIN

"Thoughts are things, my dear,"
a stranger told me in a stranger's house.
I thought of the things my thoughts
might be: after-rain from shaking
branches, tiny warped spot on a church
pew, rough shavings of a handcut picket.

Or books in other languages read
in a former life, with titles like
La Frontera de Crystal, le planetarium.

If only they could be as handsome
as the seven-hundred-year-old prayer book
of a queen, made from hand-illuminated
calf-skin parchment, the delicate opening
phrase of a violin.

When I learned the word "de minimis,"
what scientists call a risk too small
for concern, I thought of the speck
of spinach in that stranger's teeth,
tiny as the chances of being a passenger
in flames, or the girl who can't stop sneezing.

So when the custodian said I was lucky
not to have to work on Friday the 13th,
and I asked if he was superstitious
and he answered "Nah, I just don't want
nothing bad to happen to me," I understood.

Because there on the morning news
are the flames of an airplane crash, real
as hand-printed silk. Because, as a friend
once wrote, "Some things are impossible
and they come true."

ROOTWORK

A woman in a white robe stands in the almost light,
a key tucked in her pocket, clove nestled in her mouth.
She is secretary to her dreams, digging for entry,
while the nerve in her tooth blazes to its end all morning.

A key tucked in her pocket, clove nestled in her mouth,
she watches the builder pull away ceiling and leave a rise of beams
while the nerve in her roof blazes to its end all morning
and the builder mounts a new covering above the old stub.

She watches as he pulls away old ceiling and leaves a rise of beams;
pieces of decay fly back as the old surface is ground into empty space,
as the builder mounts a new covering above the old stub.
Both woman and builder stand in a maze of air and order.

Pieces of decay fly back as the old surface is ground into empty space.
A woman in a white robe stands in the almost light,
both in a maze of air, and order, in a smell a little like fire.
She is secretary to her house's dreams, digging for entry.

A SHORT TREATISE ON LOSS

There are those poems you hear about, written
in soap, veins of words washed away,
                              the shade of memory.

And that phrase you utter to yourself
with the lights out, believing, in daylight,
                              it might come back.

The dark drive to an unmarked town
to pick up a no-longer-lover at a tiny airport
                              tucked in trees,

past streets where houses
are like boxes with thin doors declaring each
                              a private universe.

The chess set Nosenko made from thread
in isolation, and his calendar of lint:
                              both taken from him.

That space in the broken-toothed smile
of a Vietnamese man I teach, who, when
                              he does not understand

a question, repeats my own words back to me
from somewhere inside the deep dark of his mouth.
                              Hello. Hello?

THE TURN

The photograph my father showed
my mother of our garden on the day
we planted it down in Florida
was an image, she said, only a real
gardener could enjoy, sensing
what the box of soil would become,
knowing the small envelopes poking
up from the earth marked places
where seeds were taking their first wide
breaths below. The way others of us know
a glass jar marked paprika contains
the burnt umber smell of grandmothers
cooking in a basement, or that around
a certain twist of road, a whole range
of blue ridges awaits. Yet the knowledge
never quite prepares us for the turn.
And as my father, my husband and I set
those seeds into their soil on the day
of planting, we might have been dropping
stars into the sky for how little we knew
of which might collapse, and which,
in that wide stretch of dark, would brighten.

DIARY OF A GARDEN WITHOUT YOU

While you were gone, I tried to grow a garden.
I wanted a ground full of plants to greet you,
pushing forward as the dog would toward the door
when you came home again,
as the four-year-olds I once taught
used to burst onto the tarred rooftop, scattering like stars.

While you were gone, I forgot to look at the stars,
and lost the book you'd gotten about gardens.
Mornings, I would wake to teach,
afternoons come home to not you,
and evenings try to cook for one again.
The dog began to sleep by the front door.

One Saturday, at last, I went out through the back door
and began to plant in the soil that sat dry under the stars
most of September, began to bring it to life again.
I started, as you'd said to, by pulling out our summer garden,
the golden cherry tomato stalks that you
and I had eaten off most of July, that month of no teaching

when we learned what wide empty days could teach
us, on some days never opening the front door.
I lowered the white threads of cucumber, wanting you
to smell this astonishing scent — already its essence, just starting
out — that would multiply its dark green through the garden,
which would fill up soon with seeds breathing below the dark again.

I watered and patted and watered again
over the next ten days, but waiting taught
me nothing — had I dug too deep or not enough? — the garden

was not growing. The scent of cucumber left completely, a door
had shut. A few beans floated to the surface, dead stars
of an empty sky. "Be patient, Grasshopper," you

told me on the phone. I tried to think of the details you
would have explained if you'd been home again
that fall, those nights we missed of walking together under stars.
I found the book I'd lost, but it could not teach
me why the seeds had not reached the door
between ground and air. I would try again to grow the garden.

The day before you returned, I set the seeds taut
in their spots again. The dog rushed to the door
and under stars, I led you to our flat, but breathing, *garden*.

CITY OF DOORS

In dreams, doors are never the point — air alone
    can keep you at as much a distance from your old love,
who sits at a party on a patio and does not see you.
    Real doors, I can't always bother to completely close —
the back door of our house in Florida, the one to my old
    bedroom in New York. Maybe I like to leave things
a little bit open, without the sound of something clicking
    closed. Maybe because I grew up in a city guarded
by heavy glass doors with gold-plated handles you had
    to use the force of your whole body to open, a city
where every morning I'd walk down a hallway of a dozen
    identical brown entrances, all closed, and ride the subway
whose doors were always sliding shut on someone.
    Once I tried to push our elevator open for the woman
who lived below us, but I didn't see her in time,
    and the door kept sliding into itself as she and I smiled
at each other with less and less of an opening,
    shrugging since there was no way we could stop it.
As there was no way, after she died inside the twin towers,
    to distinguish her door from the others beside it or from itself
the times when it was closed and she was still alive behind it.

DISCOVERY AT THE WORLD TRADE CENTER SITE

You were buried deep —
         a great ribbed ghost
in the middle of tomorrow —
         when your curved timbers,
pulled from thirty feet
         below the beaten ground,
were spotted in a backhoe.
         A team of archaeologists
identified the markings
         in your planks
as marine-nibbled signs
         that you had been
a sea-faring ship before
         you were lowered beneath
the expanding city to
         become landfill.
You, who might even
         have a name, sat
in the airless dark for
         one hundred-and-sixty years
before the towers were built,
         for the thirty that they stood,
on that Tuesday, and
         those nine years after,
as digging moved light
         closer toward you.
That Tuesday was one
         of the first days of school.
We told the children,
         startled to be woken from naps,
only that it would be
         an early day. The other
teacher and I waited until

the last child, whose mother

had walked across the

Brooklyn Bridge, went home.

And then we locked up,

entering the altered air.

To think that you, ghost,

were beneath what we saw

across the water as we

walked, beneath the smoke that was too

thick to be called smoke,

too encompassing to be a cloud,

that left ash dust on my bicycle.

As my sister stayed with me,

and we got slices of pizza

from the only place that

was open, a line around

the block. As the heels

of my downstairs neighbor

never sounded. I'd met her

only once on an ordinary

evening after her day of work

on Wall Street, but heard her

every morning getting ready.

Her name was Meredith

and she was, like me, not married.

And here I am nine years later,

standing on the beach

in St. Augustine, Florida,

with my husband of five years

whom I didn't know then.

The sand lies so flat and wide

there is space to envision

ships like you, ghost,

tilting through the waves,

arriving to explore these shores.

You, who were deep beneath

us before the falling,

when carried up in a scaffold,

began to weaken and slant

from your first contact

in two hundred years

with ordinary air, with

its brightness.

II.

A SHORT HISTORY OF LEAVENING

They say it began when Osiris decided
to lighten the weight of what we carry
from Earth to the Land of the Dead

and allowed a chance landing of wild yeast
on grain. Then, in ancient Palestine, people
threw bowls of leavening and water from houses

of mourning since the Angel of Death
was said to have left his sword inside
the potion that contained the property

of rising. Bakers in Pompeii ground millet
with must out of wine tubs and dried
the mixture in the sun, then kept it sealed

tightly in the dark. Settler fathers wrapped
pieces of previously risen dough to pass
down to marrying daughters. As I push

down the circle of dough that continues
to rise, I wonder how we learn when
to contain things, and when to let them grow.

WHAT YOU DON'T WANT TO KNOW

is what your husband now tells you
on a narrow road tucked deep in a mountain:
the speed of sound is slower than light,
which means the lightning that strikes
just to your right followed almost instantly
by a crack of thunder, is very close.
Everyone says you are safe, says if it hit,
the electrons would just flow
through the metal skin of your car.
Even the pilot who wrote a book on calm
says you may see bolts beside your plane,
but that still, real danger is very slight.
The dog hardly lifts his head from the backseat.
The cows you pass in fields of Grayson Highlands
stand poised; they know this kind of day,
familiar vibration in the ground — *So?*
Time to graze again. And your husband
likes the way driving in all kinds of weather
keeps him awake. He doesn't mind
not knowing where you'll eat or sleep
tonight, although already the dark is coming.
You think of a painter you know who is going
blind, who says in the scheme of things,
what's one old woman's eye? So why
is every bolt from the sky like a test of faith,
a scratching at your heart? Last night
when you couldn't sleep, too expectant
of disaster in the simple quiet outside the tent,
a cow mooing down by the river
reminded you that dawn was on its way again.
that the day would continue
in its worn and glorious tracks.

BETWEEN MISSING AND FOUND

We thought we knew, all week,
what was out our hotel window:
one faraway slope, buildings
piled close, wind from another
coast. It was plenty.

To think, all that while, the glistening
point of Mt. Hood rose behind
the fog, silent as light.

Seeing its pale silk appear
out our window at sunrise
on this last morning, I think
of a large poster I once
drove by, taped over a small
picture of a cat with the heading lost.
The poster shouted: WE FOUND HIM!

The joy of those capital letters
floated through me the way
this mountain appearing makes
something also like joy
course through me.

I think of when my husband
told me a car had flown through
a stop sign straight across his path,
and if he'd been half-a-second slower
in braking, he might not have made it.
He'd been saved before I knew
I had come close to losing him.

And how once I lost my grandmother's
star-of-sapphire ring, then found it
at the bottom of a small pitcher
of pencils, but kept looking for it
afterwards, without meaning to,
kept remembering its star
as something gone.

Or that young husky the color
of Mt. Hood's snow-capped peak
who landed outside my fence after
he dug out from his own. Together
we walked; I searched for any signs
of an owner looking for what he'd lost
as the dog bounded ahead, in pure whiteness,
toward whatever it was that came next.

STAYING AFLOAT AT 37,000 FEET

Myself, my legs, we tense inside
the seat, inside the flying metal
fortress with its spy-holes onto clouds,
while flight attendants — how
do they manage that daily goodbye
in a doorway between ground and sky? —
shepherd their rolling carts down
a passage lined with bulbs prepared
to light an exit through clouds of smoke
or hijackers with knives, an exit out
of any fall, as passages before
have led passengers out to sky.
But this shaking's just a wrestling
of wings against pockets of air that wend
toward us in reverse, as happens
on any journey through the sky,
though my brain still performs its own battle
against heart swell. Once I was a child
in such a seat, and lifting off land was the same
as any voyage. Once I was like the man
now beside me, who turns to his wife
in the air above a cluster of lace and asks
a question so full of simple faith I want
to weep, he asks,

       "So, what are we going to eat tonight?"

WOMAN IN A DREAM

Reader, tell me, are you, like I am, so in love
with falling asleep that you could slip
there on the hardest floor of the fastest rocking boat?

In love with that moment when arms and legs
begin unfastening and lids pull you down until
you know you are about to fall and the dark becomes
the portrait of a woman whom you've never met?

Or are you heir to an inherent restlessness, unwilling
to lose daylight? Like my hosts in Williamsburg, Virginia,
so surprised by my desire to nap rather than take
a tour around the island of Jamestown?

But, reader, it was raining, and just after lunch,
and the room I slept in faced a lake, which raindrops
dashed with their alphabet so soothingly.

And why do some of us tire so much more entirely
than others, and especially when sightseeing?

Why last week, on a visit to Charlottesville,
when my husband led me to the school playground
where once he thought he was dying, was I ready
to take a mid-morning nap on that grass?

And later, as the tour guide who led our group
in its timed procession told us the mirrors
on the walls of Monticello had never left the house,

meaning they had all reflected the face of Thomas Jefferson
multiple times into these rooms, how come I could only
think of the bed we'd just seen, designed in Paris, enclosed
by three walls and a curtain?

Think: what if I could lie there nestled in an island of history,
and for a moment not see these sights another person
might have been waiting for all of her life?

A SUDDEN DARK

Last Saturday near midnight, I watched couples
walk peacefully along First Avenue beneath the still

black sky the hour after my sister told me he had left.
Soon, the air trembled. Rain clattered

against our grandmother's terrace gate,
geraniums shook in their boxes,

the kitchen curtain swung in and out
of an open slit of window. Nothing

was gradual about this storm: couples scurried
like insects below, amid rising puddles, to escape it.

I pictured her alone across the Brooklyn Bridge
in her garden apartment: the broken

screen door slamming, the two black and white cats
pacing across the window sill, waiting

for the storm to lift,
for the night to return, still as they'd known it.

BECOMING ONE OF THEM

Because someone reminds me
  that the expression "fight or flight"
    refers to primitive times,
      when a lion chased you and you ran
        in solid fear and because the lions
      who chase us now are ethereal
    and everywhere and we drive so
  all that adrenaline ignites inside us,
I begin my jog-walking in public parks.

Because I begin these mid-afternoon
  around a lake beside a high school, I am
    the oldest person here and on my first lap
      I pass a couple standing, looking at turtles
        while holding hands; she's tall, red-haired,
        and loud, he's short, and dark, has
      a quiet, lispy voice, and by my second lap,
    they are lying in the grass, fully touching,
  the prelude over, and I remember Giancarlo
and myself in Central Park and Village View, lying
on a rubber mat below the monkey bars I grew up climbing.

Because to us it was a private place, we were who
  the park was made for; we didn't think
    of how we'd disappear to one another, didn't
      notice those jog-walking women in their thirties
        who would circle the reservoir, shaking
        hips and holding fists, the women whom
      my best friend and I used to laugh about
    as we snuck down below the jogging path,
  and waited, our skinny, unexercised legs idling,
until the rest of the class was headed back,
then pretended we had been behind them all along.

Because what moment was there to spare
  to wonder what the days of the speedwalkers
    were like, what they jogged, mid-afternoon, to dispel
  while we high-schoolers cluttered their way,
our toes tracing slow, careless circles in the ground.

ENTRY

... the only life we know is constituted by opposites.
— Anthony Storr

Doors to my rooms have lost
the power of their hinges:

    one at home swings all the way
    open at the smallest tap

and one at work lets rain slip
in through its top, leaves

    a stain in the carpet like a bruise
    that I find days later, still water

from an otherwise forgotten storm.
The way a mind swings open,

    lets things sit too long. The way
    our eyes in sleep open wide

the landing of our dreams, where doors
deceive us;

    the entrance to my grandmother's
    bedroom disappears when I want

to watch her sleep but then the front
door opens and she calls my name.

    We dance a waltz in her small living
    room. The hinges of her failing knees

become alive again. In the same sleep,
I am locked behind another door

      with an armed, well-shaven man who
      wants to harm me, who stares into my eyes

and says that he will haunt my dreams.
Our eyelids lift us back from sleep,

      but still we see that mirror to a world
      where dark and light can steal through any door.

EVEN IN CLEAR AIR

The bales of hay are wet from last night's rain
and the damp air that followed it
has shifted to brisk currents stirring sunlight.

We wanted to see the cows
asleep last night, so we walked through the wet dark,
eyes adjusting to silhouettes.

Twice you said you saw a shooting star
but twice I missed it. There are moments
in marriage you cannot share, and moments you must —

the bed unmade, a curtain
falling off its hook, a rattle of breath
that startles even the snorer.

These sounds, once learned, become the soft sputters
of a lake, what bark might say
if it spoke. There's a joy to not knowing whether the shape

on top of a faraway mountain is a column or a cloud.

FIRST GARDEN

Bending over soil in the spring
with my new mother-in-law,
planting two rows of sunflowers
and three of corn, it comes to me —
that the words *wedding* and *weeding*
are only a letter apart,

that I've never been in charge
of a garden, or even been good
at remembering to water
plants inside, to keep them
where they'd get the light
they needed.

I think of my mother, mornings
in a new country setting,
so content to be nestled among rows
of blossoming asparagus,
her blue starchy gloves tearing up
each slender green invader by its roots.

She liked to say she was
cleaning what she could,
unlike my father's mounds
of newspapers, an office chair
found on the sidewalk, coffee
grounds spilling onto the floor.

When my mother-in-law and I
step back from the faceless garden,
and she says, "Ok, now grow!"

her palms in giddy fists, I feel
the charge of this, the hand I'll need
to give to tidy this little patch of
things that might be about to happen.

THROUGH ELEMENTS

With goggles on, I look into nothing that is clear —
a cloud of lake dust, a clump of water vine
that floats in formless space, much colder here,
when legs dip deeper, as though they fall through time.
I turn to say we should swim over to that tree.
You hesitate, but I reply it's not so far.
So we swim, my love, and, oh, the water's sweet
as it slips inside my mouth, as my arms carve
glorious hollows through the pond. Until
I glimpse you climb with rough breath out the side.
How could I be thinking all the while,
sweet water when you, just behind, my guide
on land, as much my element as breath, felt fear?
As I, with goggles on, looked into nothing clear.

A KNOB, A POST, A SCATTERING

My husband tore our kitchen down to the studs,
    making it a chasm in our house,
        dark breath of wood:
    a room is stripped before a room is built.

He suffered warm air slipping through plywood
    and blasted off wall, drilling like a wild
        dentist, pulling hard on what did not want
    to be let loose, screws gripping to their space

like cats' claws: things stick, tongue in groove.
    The way plaster dust and cantaloupe rind studding
        the floor stuck to our feet so that we,
    horses trotting through our pasture,

spread our traces everywhere. I read in *The Anatomy*
    of a Wall that a jack stud is the post
        that transfers the load of a wall
    and that the king is placed above, to support

the whole assembly. Is beside them, then, the queen?
    Regarding in green flip-flops, washing dishes
        in her bathtub, in this hour studded
    with commotion. This hour before we'll land again

on two sides of a window. I'll hold onto the pane
    while you shimmy in the frame, as we begin
        again to build, to stay:
    something hidden holds us up.

WE ARE PASSING OVER

after Edward Hirsch's "For the Sleepwalkers"

This morning before sunrise, a man
who must dream of air and drop his sleep
to study maps of sky, keeps the cabin

dark for sleepers, the only sound
a little humming of the clouds. He speaks
certainties of time and distance

in a voice so even it releases that other
story, imagined, from my throat, and leads
us lightly, safely, back to ground.

As the line of us waits to exit, soon
to board other planes that stand at their gates
like reliable horses, I think the quick thanks

I'll give is not enough. No, today, to the man
who carries me over the city where I was born
so that I am nothing but a speck above

my parents' home, which is itself a speck beneath
the skyscrapers, tallest blocks of tin foil
beside a box of green that must be Central Park,

each place becoming, at this distance, its essence,
I want to say: *O seer of the great open, you show us our old*
lives through the scope of air and riverbed, your motors stir

mystery warm as cows' milk, wings whir our bodies
in an arc from ground to ground. If only we
could slip this way, from cloud to delicate cloud,

in increments of city to city. If only we could learn
to pass over and back like this, to find, amid
any condition of landscape, the right way to go home.

APARTMENT

What did my father do
with the dead hamsters,
the gerbils we let
loose in the bathtub?
Where tonight my teenage
nieces will bathe. Tonight
they'll sleep on the broken
springs of the sofa bed
and wake to breakfast
with their mother
at the round table
in its corner of sky,
where my sister and I used to
argue over who went where.

The table on which my father
once left a note that said
he would be very disappointed
if I chose what I chose:
to spend the night away.
My father was like a moth
to me then, wings clutching
and folded, holding
to the window: morning, night.

The table my mother stood
at in her underwear, leaning
her head out to wash
the windows fourteen stories
high while Bob Dylan blared.
Where my grandfather sat
in a cone birthday hat each May.

Table with dark streaks, waxy
to the touch, chosen before
I was born. Behind it
is the window with glimpses
of a concrete whale, treetops
and the Empire State Building.

Tonight I stand at the counter
of my new kitchen in Florida,
looking out clean windows.
Mushrooms spring up like
parachutes along the green
planets of silence that in the city
would be lost in a swell of inhabitants.

My mother's kitchen was never large.
Decades pass in it like water boiling,
then cooling down. I stand at my counter,
afraid to make those first marks, to taint
the unstained page of wood.

EARLY NOTE

Elevated lights
beside a pool where
early risers swim
are like our dreams:
soon to go out but
still buzzing in the dark.

Arms glide through water
in this almost-light
the way I wish a mind
could move, steady
in space, through to the
next stretch of open
lane ahead.

In this hum before
the dawn,
the day's already
drawn itself on one
more continent,
has already witnessed
the end of what it started,
and still begins again.

THROUGH A NEW WINDOW

I can hear the three men who built
this room praying on the back porch,
their voices the sign of another day rising.

I know they're standing in a circle
holding hands beside my bicycle,
draped with a dirty pink towel,

behind the cooler whose moldy corners
hide a key to the house, because
they've done this every morning

for the last half a year they've worked here.
First they pull up in large white trucks
scaring sparrows into their little house

as my husband or I announce to the
other, "They're here." Then they pray
as we peek through a curtain, and then

begin their work. This window a month ago
was still a square in wood. Doors without knobs
leaned against the wall like pieces

of a broken drawbridge. Voices and the sound
of men building often sailed through the window
of my childhood apartment, from other blocks or stories.

But none so quiet, so close as this — a prayer
climbing up new screen, the man I love knocking
on our own panes of fresh glass.

MONSOON IN MAINE

All afternoon — over the clearing
    and assembly, the poles and cloth
        that four of us held above the two
            whose lives were being joined —

it waited; waited while a glass was broken
    and the flock of us who faced the Atlantic
        from the green were summoned out
            of brokenness toward repair;

waited when we recessed toward the barn
    and held out arms for one another
        as we stepped over roots rising.
            Perhaps then a parade of almost drops

readied themselves to land, for soon a few
    slipped lightly into pots of hollowed bark,
        around edges of footprints, trying them on.
            Maybe this was a new rain that didn't know

about the rush of needing to fall. Or maybe
    there's no other way for a rain to begin;
        slight and then unstoppable,
            seeping back into loosened earth,

spilling through edges of tent, falling
    over voices calling out in celebration
        until the rains themselves were part
            of what we praised.

How like a marriage was the night
   of dancing with feet wet enough to slip,
      hands lifting beside the tempo, ever shifting,
         of this great continued sound of pouring down.

REMODELING

My house is a broken bone,
its walls sigh me goodnight in their old age,
the shower pours its icy offering down cracked tiles,
and attic steam, that scent of suitcase, old pieces
of an old life, slips down a slit of bead board.

I still have dreams I'm living in Brooklyn
on a top floor apartment, where snow
on skylights made a wall of light
between two young women, uncertain
what to do in the city, and the sky;

we were girls grown in a room of girls
who stayed where we thought we belonged.
"D'accord, d'accord," we chanted
with Madame Kohler in the mansion
of our dirty shoes and cotton skirts rolled high,
bodies beneath an intricate ship of eaves
and ridge lines, climbing up twisted marble stairs.

This morning, on the sill of a new window
beside a door sealed for what may have been
thirty years inside a wall resting on broken piers
sat a little yellow dump truck,
wheels pointed forward, circled
by dust-glittered bobby pins,
the bones of another life.

ALIGHT

Born in a city where we couldn't see the stars,
I draped my window in diamond bulbs above scents
of burritos and curry, bars' flocks of late night voices
lifting up those fourteen flights from Sixth street,
corner of my first kiss, slow slope of tasted light
below a sky of copper domes and endless roofs,
timed galaxy where clumps of skyscraper turned black
at midnight and sidewalks never slept.
I slipped into this staccato light not knowing
I'd land a thousand miles South, under canopies
of Spanish moss, on a runway of fireflies.
Tonight, beside a dark lake, I watched a woman
sit in her car and turn on the interior light;
how that one bulb shone like a tiny planet.

POEM OF LOST LINES

There's the kind of silence that comes after a television breaks,
when its picture turns to blackness and the track of laughter
that had just been lulling us to sleep becomes a crackle of burnt cord.

And the kind that lies in the space around the yellow belly
of a dead bird, a body that had been all song, swept beside the curb.
Once I wrote about goldenrod pushing up after a short sleep

in its valley, compared the sky to a slate marked with claps
of eraser's chalk, described how my dog was always barking
at a remnant of sound just outside the fence, though I did not manage

to describe the remnant. None of these lines lived in their songs.
And maybe that's the saddest thing about silence — we never know
what else might have filled it, and we aren't allowed to choose

everything that stays. Those bells in an oak leaf hydrangea
like feather paper, a husband's accidental memory for landscape
and the colors of doors — these may not have been the right pieces

to fill a certain empty track, though they fall easily there,
like old petals. Maybe I should have ended here, but I want
to keep on going, because the morning of my sister's wedding,

I watched boats cross New York's Harbor, a timeless part
of the city, and I didn't know if those white tips of waves
were part of the foam of ocean or birds in a family at a distance,

lightly tossed and swimming. But as I prepared my toast,
I found the words I'd chosen, though they could have been
many other things, slipped through my lips like water.

TO WALK A FAMILIAR ROUTE IN REVERSE

It's what you know from a former sea.
The house that hid behind you to the right
slips into view — turquoise, grand.

The flatnesses that followed curves
come first now; this shifts the angle

of your self to sky, and is a way you never —
is a blurred new broken shore.

If you think you are wise in this age,
goes the bible verse, *you should
become fools so you may become wise.*

Does this mean — study your dog as he
pulls apart a branch and chews,

highest praise for flavors of smoked
earth, a taste of sky? Take one broken thing inside?

The blossoms, you wrote, *have suddenly appeared,*
yet all winter they have been preparing to rise.
You are the one slow to uncover.

Slow to sing, be still enough to wade
through the dark and flowers.

UNPLOTTED

One woman leaned
over another on the shoulder
of the road. A thin black
sweater fluttered backward.
Whatever had happened
had just happened.
Trucks piled up
behind us, a procession
for the woman none of us knew.
And in this curve of dust
and sky, on Route 62-180
to El Paso, beside a mountain
where that morning
we'd risen in the wind,
where somewhere close a border
had been drawn,
we waited and were told
the wait would be long.
Men stood in clumps,
speaking Spanish, taking turns
to walk out to the desert
and relieve themselves, glance
through swaying brush
at the afterwards ahead,
wives still in their passenger seats
with the doors nudged open.
Such an easy thing,
to wait, to be alive, but
some of us closed our eyes
and sighed. How soon,
we wanted to know, could
we be back on the road like those

who would come upon this curve
in a few hours and pass over it,
as they'd pass over any other
spot along their way, not knowing?

LAST BREATH

I got out of bed
on two strong legs.
It might have been
otherwise.
         — Jane Kenyon

Last night, as I turned my body
into its curve of sleep, my husband
still awake, erasing dust from digital
negatives in the other room,
a warning sounded six miles from Buffalo
to alert the crew their aircraft might be
about to lose its lift and fall out of the sky.
The passengers — alive when I drifted
to sleep, pushing seat backs into their upright
positions, returning books to bags —
were not alive when I awoke, like
any other morning, mind first, then eyes
opening to light green walls, arms
and legs beginning to move again.
My husband turned on the TV —
an airplane ablaze — and turned it off
before, he thought, I could see.
In *The Spirit of St. Louis*, Lindbergh describes
how he waited, restless, in New York
for the weather to be right for his take-off
to Paris, how he tried going to movies
to lose himself in the story, but how
all he could see on the screen were wings
and engines turning, inner organs of rods
and sparks, pistons reversing themselves
at incomprehensible speeds. I see fallen
wings behind the screens of possibilities.

Over and over I read — "our hearts go out,
our deepest sympathies'" — and think
of the plane trying to gain speed
with its nose down, how stick shaker
rattled yoke to return control to the hands
of the pilot in that stretch of sky
where twenty-seven minutes later another
airplane flew and landed without incident.
This morning, as I lift one leg behind me,
lean my torso forward, arms stretched
out like wings, trying not to think of all
the weight entrusted to one foot,
light shakes from the sky, tilts through
the window pane and, oh, my heart goes out.

NOTES

The quotation from Pablo Neruda in "Courting, Paynes Prairie" is from "Epithalamium " in *The Captain's Verses*, translated by Donald Walsh.

The form of "On Forgetting You Might Need a Ride" is based on the poem "Who Cares About Aperture?" from *And Her Soul Out of Nothing* by Olena Kalytiak Davis.

The poem title, "Symphony in the Brain," is taken from the book title, *A Symphony in the Brain: The Evolution of the New Brain Wave Biofeedback,* by Jim Robbins. The quotation in the last line of the poem is from "Accident" in *Body of the World* by Sam Taylor.

In "Discovery at the World Trade Center Site," the italics in the second and third lines are from the article, "18th Century Ship Found at Trade Center Site," by David W. Dunlap in *The New York Times*, July 14, 2010. His line reads: "In the middle of tomorrow, a great ribbed ghost has emerged from a distant yesterday."

"Monsoon in Maine" is dedicated to Maura and Rufus.

ABOUT THE AUTHOR

Christine Poreba's work has appeared in *The Southern Review, The Sun Magazine, Subtropics, The Pinch* and other publications. In addition to the Philip Levine Prize for Poetry, she is the recipient of a Florida Individual Artist Fellowship and a Dorothy Sargent Rosenberg Poetry Prize. A native New Yorker, she currently lives in Tallahassee, Florida with her husband, son, and dog. She teaches English as a Second Language to adults. *Rough Knowledge* is her first book.

ROUGH KNOWLEDGE
POEMS BY CHRISTINE POREBA

There is an extraordinary lightness to this collection of poems — it is as if they are floating just above the surface of the earth, or in dream, as they celebrate love, marriage, family, friends — the small accidents and genuine delights of everyday life. The poems are filtered through a sweet and deeply thoughtful sensibility. You will grow to love the narrator of these poems as she leads us, bravely and with caritas, to the threshold of things, frightening or heavenly, "that might be about to happen." Christine Poreba's debut collection is radiantly lovely.

> — *Sidney Wade*

We begin Christine Poreba's new book with a small miracle: a dead horseshoe crab who turns out not to be dead, but to move "like a speeding turtle, a dusty shoe with legs," and we realize that we are in the presence of a poet whose eye and ear we immediately trust. *Rough Knowledge* is a book we come to count on for its insight and its appreciation for the tonal resonances of our language. It offers us vowels and consonants doing what they do best: giving us a world to inhabit, one of sudden catastrophe and equally surprising delights, snow-covered Brooklyn skylights, gardens, soffits, jack studs, and dogs running toward "whatever it was that came next." It's not just a brave book, but a wise one.

> — *Christopher Bursk*

In *Rough Knowledge*, Christine Poreba has a poem in which she says, " I want them both:/ the space, the containment." That desire is familiar, I think, to most of us. Not incidentally, however, it also is at the heart of making poems, certainly Poreba's poems, which begin in some common event or scene — flying a model plane, watching someone familiar walk down a street at night — only to lead into a restless questioning of what appeared as common. Hers is a beautifully sustained and often surprising art of connections that takes nothing for granted. Even a butterfly's sudden smear across a windshield "could/ look a bit like/any human sorrow …" I don't mean to suggest that her poems move toward abstraction or conclude in comforting generalities. She has an eye for exact particulars and doesn't stray from them, but her poems are so transparent, so quiet and intimate with the daily ambiguities and revelations of experience, that if you listen carefully you can almost believe the movement within her poems is like breathing: inward-containment, outward-space. I want such poetry close at hand.

> — *Peter Everwine, Judge — Philip Levine Prize for Poetry*

$20
Anhinga Press
P.O. Box 3665
Tallahassee, FL 32315
www.anhinga.org

ISBN 978-1-934695-47-0

5 2 0 0 0